Heavenly Grief

A Christian Guide To Spiritual and Emotional Healing

By Don and Karen Clifford

What others are saying about Heavenly Grief

Robert D. (Bob) Nowlin, MSW, D.Min
Chaplain of Unity Hospice of Greater St Louis.

I heartily endorse this book as helpful to anyone who wants to address grief from a Christian perspective. As a Hospice Chaplain for over six years and a minister and social worker for over forty years, I can say this work is one of the more practical and beneficial books on grief I have read. I can recommend it for use by individuals in the midst of, or preparing for, grief and for those helping others cope with grief. I also can see it being used as a study guide for grief support groups or seminars. I know I can use it in my hospice ministry.

My wife, Jean, and I have known Don and Karen and their family for over forty years, and I can testify that what is expressed in this book is not theoretical for them, but it comes out of who and what they are as a result of their life experiences, struggles, and triumphs rooted in their relationships to God through Jesus Christ. This small book should be a "must read" for all persons because we all will experience grief in our lives and can benefit from this simple and insightful guide for dealing with our grief from a Christian perspective."

Pastor Craig Atherton, M.Div
Trinity Baptist Church, Wichita, KS

I would like to recommend this book not only for its content, but for its intent. My sister and brother-in-law authored this book. Therefore, I was able to witness firsthand through the years the reality in their lives of what they write in this book. To see the faith, hope, and love that permeated through each of the trials of this couple was a source of tremendous strength for me. You will be blessed by the insights learned and shared, and will be encouraged as you read how God sustained them each step of the way. Anyone who has had to endure a tragic loss, or knows of someone who has to whom they can minister, will benefit greatly from this book.

Table Of Contents

Introduction

In our companion book entitled "Grace Enough for Three" we tell the story of our family's struggles during the loss of three of our children. We are life-long Christians and while our faith was tested severely, God was faithful, and as he promised, he never left us nor did he forsake us. We found that his grace is always sufficient, hence the title of the companion book. It's not our purpose to discuss our family's losses here, except to quickly summarize what happened so the reader will have enough knowledge of our experiences to understand our perspective on the work of grief.

Our tragedies began when Michael, our second child, suffered from brain seizures and died when he had a seizure and suffocated in his bedding during the night. He was two and a half years old. We had moved to California after graduating from college in Kansas, where our first child, Vicki, was born. After losing Mike, we packed up and moved back to the Midwest to be nearer family and friends. A few years later, after two miscarriages and the birth of our second daughter, Becky, our third daughter was born. Rachel was a beautiful, normal baby, but she contracted spinal meningitis at the age of three months. She survived, but only in a badly brain-damaged state. She lived for a few years but we never knew if she could even see or hear. She required constant care, and we finally lost her when her little body gave out when she was three and a half years old. Then our last child, Beth, developed the same seizure disorder that her brother had several years before. She was 5 years old, sweet, beautiful and full of life. While we were out one night, we left Beth with her 13 year-old sister Becky. Beth suffered a seizure while alone in a shallow bathtub, and in the few minutes it took Becky to find her, she was unconscious. Becky called 911 but Beth had been without oxygen for too long, and after a few days in ICU she died and left us all in a state of shock.

Through the experiences of losing Michael, Rachel and Beth, we suffered much pain and were at times distressed, confused and dismayed by what was happening to our family. As life-long Christians and Bible teachers, we sought comfort and guidance from the Holy Spirit and the Word of God through those dark days. The observations and conclusions we share in this book are simply testimonies of how God has dealt with us, shaped us, and we believe, even spoken to us through our experiences. They are hopefully validated to some degree by the survival of our faith and our resultant walk with God.

All of these tragedies took place over a period of almost twenty years, during which time, through God's grace, our family maintained our devotion to God and trusted in him completely to see us through the ordeals. Today, our surviving family, and now our grandchildren, are happy and whole and praising God for his infinite grace.

As I said before, the purpose of this smaller book is not to dwell on our family's experiences, except to occasionally illustrate a point using specific events in our lives. We only relate this much of our story to establish that we have been through the grief process, not once, but several times. Not only that, but we also dealt with an endless stream of doctors, hospitals, seizures and three years with a brain-damaged child. We have also read, and are familiar with the generally accepted teachings on the psychology of grief. However, most of that literature we have seen was written from a theoretical viewpoint or by outside observers.

As a result of our multiple experiences we began to learn some other things about surviving grief that aren't covered in the text books. We learned how to survive our losses and how to recover in a reasonable time, not by our own effort, but rather by learning to avail ourselves of God's provisions. Certainly, a big part of that provision was the strong Christian upbringing each of our families' gave us. We thank God and give him praise for giving us that preparation.

The focus of this book is how we accessed God's provisions for dealing with grief, and the principles behind them.

Much of the material in this little book is also contained in "Grace Enough for Three", but here we are concentrating on the recovery process. The spiritual lessons to be learned can help us go on to a full and happy life in a reasonable time.

We have found that when some people are dealing with the death of a loved one, they are not interested in reading about someone else's grief. When we tried to share with them the material from Grace Enough For Three, they weren't up to reading it. However, we have also found that the same people were usually open to counsel and advice as to what they can expect and how they can best get through the grief process. When we shared the material in Heavenly Grief with them, they thanked us and told us it was very helpful. That is why we decided to pull some of the relevant material from "Grace" and produce this book.

We have written this book from a Christian perspective because that's the only perspective that we know. If you have a background in the faith you will hopefully understand and appreciate it, but it will not spare you the pain of your loss. That pain is an essential part of your grieving process. However, we hope it will help you to move through the process more quickly and avoid unnecessary pitfalls that can trap you in distress, and possibly even lead you into clinical depression.

You do not have to be a Christian to benefit from what is shared in this book. We think the principles discussed will be easily understood and found to be of benefit to anyone experiencing a significant loss. In the process we pray this book will help you to a new and rewarding relationship with God. We pray that the Lord will bless you as you read and as you share this little book with people you care about who are suffering through the grief process. You will find that his grace is indeed sufficient.

The Compassion of God

Through all of our family's losses, we have come to the conclusion that along with love, grief is surely the deepest and most profound of all human emotions. In a real sense, grief is the flip side of love. The two are closely intertwined because without love there would be no grief. The fact we allowed ourselves to love someone makes the work of grief necessary when we lose them. The greater the love, the deeper the sorrow, and the longer it will take to work through it. As Joy says in "C. S. Lewis Through the Shadowlands", [1] "That's the deal!"

We were created by a God who loves us. We know that he cares about us personally. He knows exactly how our emotions work so he knows how deeply we hurt when we lose a loved one. God loves each one of his children and he lets us know that when a Christian dies, it is a big deal in heaven. Psalms 116:15 says, *"Precious to the Lord is the death of one of his saints."* But he also cares about those of us left behind. Among the wonderful beatitudes of Jesus in Matthew 5 is verse 4, which says *"Blessed are those who mourn, for they* **shall** *be comforted."* The common theological interpretation of this beatitude is that what Jesus meant to say is that when we mourn for our sinful condition, we will be comforted by God's forgiveness. That's a fair and reasonable interpretation, and it's obviously true. However, Jesus' words can surely be taken literally also. Because grief is perhaps the most profound experience of life, God makes this blessing available to his children who are in sorrow. Yes, people just like us who have recently lost loved ones can claim this promise; we *shall* be comforted. The promise in itself is a great comfort to those of us in grief because it reminds us that God knows our pain and he suffers with us. His compassion is infinite, so he not only cares about our grief, he is going to do something about it. He knows all of us will eventually have to face the experience of mourning and grief. Therefore, in his great wisdom and compassion he has made provision for us to be comforted. That provision may come through family, church, friends, the Bible, or just through the personal ministry of the Holy Spirit.

You may wonder how we can know for sure that the Lord really feels our pain. One of Karen's dearest verses in the Bible is Romans 8:32, which says *"God did not spare his own Son, but gave him up for us all—how will he not also along with him, graciously give us all things?"* God experienced the same grief we have experienced, only to a much greater degree. Giving up a part of himself to be humiliated and tortured, and even hung on a disgraceful cross to die while people looked on and taunted him, had to be the hardest thing God ever did. So, if he loved us enough to go through that agony, he certainly loves us enough to care for us when we suffer.

Another indication that God feels our pain is in the life and ministry of Jesus Christ. Jesus modeled for us the very character of God. Jesus said, *"I do nothing on my own, but speak just what the Father has taught me." John 8:28.* He also said, *"If you have seen me, you have seen the Father" John 14:9.* By observing the compassion of Jesus, we see the compassion of the Father. God does care about us and his heart aches for us in our grief. We can see this in John, Chapter 11, where Jesus tarried when the news of his friend Lazarus' illness reached him. By the time he arrived at the home of Mary and Martha, Lazarus had been dead for four days. Martha surely felt betrayed by the Lord. She said, *"Lord if you had been here, my brother would not have died."* She was blaming God for her brother's death, and she was probably right. If the Lord had been there, he most likely would have healed Lazarus, rather than just letting him die in his presence. However, Jesus had a purpose for letting his friend die at that particular time, just as we're sure he had a purpose for taking our loved ones when and how he did. Of course, in our minds there is never a good time for a loved one to die unless they are undergoing prolonged suffering. However, death will visit all of us somewhere along life's path. It's just a matter of when. In the case of Lazarus, we get to see the reason why he died when he did.

Before Jesus revealed his plan to Martha and Mary, he saw the intense pain and grief in their hearts. They loved their brother deeply and didn't understand why he had to die. Jesus understood the confusion and feelings of betrayal they were experiencing. His heart grieved for them to the point that he personally groaned repeatedly in his own Spirit. And then... "*Jesus wept*". Why? He knew he would soon restore their brother to them and everything would be fine. But, he groaned because he knew and felt the pain in their hearts, and his compassion for these loved ones caused him to weep and grieve with them in that moment of their pain. The Lord knew that in just a few moments they would be experiencing great joy. Still, he wept, feeling with them the sorrow in their hearts.

We can relate this reaction of our Lord to our own experience. Each time a friend or family member came to be with us after one of our children had died, there would always be a new round of tears as we embraced and shared our sorrow. Even as I (Don) stood by and watched as someone came in and embraced Karen and they cried together, I would feel my own emotions swell again, and I would weep with them. The sharing of sorrow in this way is a very normal and very healthy thing to do and I think Jesus in his humanity felt the same emotions.

Then Jesus performed what was perhaps his most remarkable miracle as he called loudly into the tomb, *"Lazarus, come forth"*. Jesus raised Lazarus from the dead after four days. Yes, Jesus even revealed the reason for Lazarus' death as he prayed to the Father audibly *"...that the people may believe that you sent me."* Jesus feels your pain too, and he weeps for each of us in our sorrow, even though he knows the future will be better than the present as he works out his perfect plan for our lives. He has promised that when we are grieved, he will help us to endure because we shall be comforted. That knowledge provides a good starting point for us as we face the struggle ahead.

In 2 Corinthians the Apostle Paul waxes eloquently about God's comforting grace. He says, *"Praise be to the God and Father of our Lord Jesus Christ, the Father of compassion and the God of all comfort, who comforts us in all our troubles, so that we can comfort those in any trouble with the comfort we ourselves have received from God."* 2 *Corinthians 1:3-5*. First of all, God comforts us in our afflictions. What a privilege to be ministered to by the Father of compassion and all comfort. After we are comforted, and presumably after we have recovered sufficiently, then it will be our turn to be the instrument of God's compassion as we pass on his comfort to others who are suffering. As a result of what you have gone through you will feel more compassion and empathy for others who are suffering and they will be better able to accept your comfort. But first, we ourselves need to openly and gladly receive his compassion and comfort as we proceed through our time of grieving.

Comfort From God's Family

When our son Mike died, we were living with Mike and our first child, Vicki, in Southern California. We had lived there three years but had no Christian neighbors and not been able to get into regular attendance in a church, so we hadn't connected with anyone as close personal friends. After Mike's death, we called the First Baptist Church in Van Nuys where we had been attending and they sent a staff minister over to visit us. We don't even remember his name. He appeared to be a pleasant and caring person, and he brought us a lovely book of poems, trying to give us some words of comfort. He seemed uncomfortable trying to minister to us when he didn't know us, but at least someone came. A couple of our neighbors stopped by to express their sympathy, and Don's aunt and her husband from across the valley came over to be with us that first evening. Otherwise, we were isolated and alone. We needed our family and we needed someone who loved us and understood our grief to be there for us.

When Mike died, the trauma was excruciating. The grief and sorrow of his loss overwhelmed us and we wanted to get back to Kansas and be with our families as quickly as possible. We needed them and we wasted no time deciding to take Mike's body back home to Kansas for burial. Don had already been looking for a job back in the Midwest so we were sure we wouldn't be staying much longer in California. We made the arrangements to have Mike's body flown to Kansas, then made travel arrangements to get our little family home. When we returned after the funeral, it was to an empty and lonely house, filled with memories of Mike. But we were alone; no one came by to see us.

Looking back now, when we compare that situation with the support we received years later from our church in Missouri, it makes us realize how important it is to belong to a community of believers. It was our own fault we hadn't gotten ourselves more involved with the church in California, but in our immaturity, we just couldn't find a place where we felt comfortable. We were also concerned that Mike's seizures would prevent us from leaving him in the nursery at church with people we didn't know.

So, while the church as an institution tried to minister to us through a sympathetic gesture, we realize now it is the people, not the institution, that ministers to people in emotional need. Comfort is ministered best through close personal relationships. People care about you when you are a part of their lives. We were not part of anyone's lives there in California when Mike died, and as a result we had only each other to lean on.

Soon after Mike's death, we found an opportunity to move back to the Midwest to be nearer family and a more compatible culture. It was a few years after getting settled in the St. Louis area that we had our second tragic loss. The experience of losing Mike in California stands in stark contrast to the situation in Missouri where we became a close and integral part of the church family. We developed many close personal friends, but in reality the entire church was our family. We were still a few hundred miles away from our closest biological family members but our church family was there for us when we needed them. When our daughters Rachel and Beth died, our home was full of people during the days leading up to the funeral, most of whom brought food, and it was like a party. Instead of playing games we sat around in groups, some on the furniture, but many on the floor, and we talked about the child we had lost. There was a lot of crying, but there was also laughing as we remembered some of the humorous events of their lives. Bottom line: they showered us with love and comfort; they were there for us, and that made our loss much less painful.

The memorial services that were held for each of the girls we lost were packed out. The church was full and the music, testimonies and encouragement ministered to us in wonderful ways. People came by afterwards and hugged us and gave us love and support that touched our souls. We feel so sorry for people who have to go through the loss of a loved one without people like that to lean on. We firmly believe that part of what Jesus had in mind when he said *"Blessed are they that mourn, for they shall be comforted"* was the support and ministry of family and friends, especially those who have the same heartbeat for the Lord as the one who is being comforted. Many of them have lost someone also. So, while you may feel alone in your grief, you can know that many people have gone down this path before you, and they understand what you are feeling. Therefore they are able to comfort you with the comfort they received when they were grieving.

Most people have some close friends or neighbors, even if they don't have family around. However, if you don't have anyone close to you, that probably means you are not active in a local church. May we suggest that if you don't have a local church family, you go find one. One of the functions of the Christian church is to love and support one another in times of need. Many churches have grief support groups and they are helpful to many people. Grief support groups can also be located through hospital chaplains and some community centers.

Comfort From God's Word

How else does God comfort us? He may do it through others, but others can't always be there when we need them. Thankfully, he will also minister to us through his Word if we will avail ourselves of it. The Bible, God's inspired Word, is in itself a wonderful source of comfort. Both of us have a very high regard for the Scriptures as the inspired Word of God. We know from experience that the teachings of the Bible can be trusted to provide guidance and strength through every experience in life, no matter how difficult that experience may be. Time and time again God has used the Scriptures to speak to our family and give us peace, comfort, assurance and strength through all of our trials. The Bible is replete with passages addressed specifically to the grieving soul. Our family found refuge in the wonderful, blessed words as we spent much time… countless hours, soaking up the precious words of Holy Scripture. We entreat you to find comfort in God's Word.

If you are not familiar with the Bible and need some guidance about where to look for comfort, let us suggest a few passages to get you started. First of all, there are the words of Jesus to his disciples as he was preparing to leave them. Read chapters 14 through 17 of the book of John in the New Testament. You may get caught up in what's happening in that passage and read clear on through the rest of the book. There are many Psalms which speak poetically to the soul. The most famous is the 23rd Psalm, but you might also read Psalms 13, 23, 34, 42, 103 and 109:73-80. There are many others of course, but as you read these you will revel in God's love and provision for you and for all his children. Back in the New Testament again, we suggest the book of Philippians, but especially the 4th chapter. Besides the Philippians, the Apostle Paul obviously loved the people in the Thessalonica church very much, His words to them in both books (1st and 2nd Thessalonians) are full of pathos as he prepares to leave them, and later as he writes to them expressing his love and his desire to see them again. Chapter 4 of the book of 1 John talks about the active love of God, but First Corinthians 13 is called the "Love Chapter" of the Bible. Actually, you don't have to search far in any part of the Bible, but especially the New Testament, to find words of comfort and assurance.

Karen's faith was tried to the maximum when Beth died. In addition to the cumulative effect of our previous losses, her life had been totally wrapped up in Beth. At that time our other daughters were teenagers and were involved with their own friends and activities. Karen had never worked outside the home. Her entire married life had been spent raising her children with their special problems. In the years before Beth began school, it was just Karen and Beth alone together during the day.

When Beth's seizure disorder became known, Karen felt the Lord gave her a promise from Isaiah 43:18-19 where it was written, *"Forget the former things; do not dwell on the past. See, I am doing a new thing!"* Karen interpreted this verse as a promise from the Lord that Beth wouldn't suffer the same fate as her brother Mike. She took strength from that verse and was encouraged that the Lord would protect Beth from harm.

Then, when Beth died, Karen was crushed. She thought God had promised her Beth would not die. Disillusionment and doubt were piled on top of the sorrow of her loss. She was confused. She wondered if she had just found a verse in the Bible that told her what she wanted to hear? Had God led her down the primrose path? The spiritual dilemma multiplied her pain. She didn't lose faith in God, but she felt she had been let down by him and her pain was severe.

It is to Karen's credit that she always goes back to God and his Word for the answer to her distress. She searched the Bible daily, reading and waiting for God to speak and tell her what he was doing and why this terrible thing had happened. She wanted and needed an answer. Then, finally, God spoke to her. However, it was not to answer all of her questions, but simply to give her a beautiful word of encouragement to just trust him. She found the words that satisfied her need in the inspired words of the prophet Habbakuk.

"Though the fig tree does not bud and there are no grapes on the vines, though the olive crop fails and the fields produce no food, though there are no sheep in the pen and no cattle in the stalls, Yet I will rejoice in the Lord, I will be joyful in God my savior. The Sovereign Lord is my strength." Habbakuk 3:17

The prophet Habakkuk understood the character of God. He recognized God as perfectly holy and pure and one who can do no wrong, even though circumstances make it appear that he has deserted us. Our all-loving and holy God could never be the source of sin or error. Therefore, whatever God decides to do is the correct, perfect and proper course of action, even if it requires us to experience difficulties and temporary pain. Our tiny brains can never begin to comprehend the complexities of God's plans. We can't see beyond the present moment. On the other hand, God knows the future in the context of eternity. It has been said that we would choose the same course for our lives as God has, if we knew everything he knows.

The faith of Habakkuk did not require the circumstances be pleasant before he could trust God. Through his inspired words Karen came to that same position. Her trust and faith in God could not be based upon external circumstances, even if those circumstances included losing three of her children. She drew strength from the assurance in that passage that God is in control and his unbounded love for us will carry us through any and all disasters. She knew now she could and would love him and trust him, no matter what. And it wasn't just an intellectual answer. God's Holy Spirit used that verse to open her to the embrace of the Father. She was buoyed and comforted in her spirit through God's promise to her. I (Don) am so blessed to have such a strong woman of faith as my wife. She gave strength to me when I should have been giving strength to her.

Both Karen and Habakkuk came to understand that no matter what calamity befalls us, we must trust God and rejoice in his goodness and his care for us. He has promised us, as a minimum, that tribulations will produce Godly character in us that he can use if we will persevere. He has also promised us that our current sufferings are nothing compared with the glories awaiting us in heaven. Another precious verse in Romans 8 speaks of this reality. *"I consider that our present sufferings are not worth comparing with the glory that will be revealed in us…. But, we ourselves, who have the first fruits of the Spirit, groan inwardly as we wait eagerly for our adoption as sons, the redemption of our bodies." Romans 8:18,23*

It is so like God to lead us individually to him by the path that works uniquely for us. With Don, it was through the ancient book of Job, written over three thousand years ago. The book of Job was especially meaningful to Don after Beth died. He read it not just once, but over and over again. It helped because he could see how his pain was reflected in Job's experience and in his words. Don could relate to Job's confusion and consternation after his multiple losses. But more importantly, he could see how God could be working in our situation to accomplish a similar objective.

The Bible tells us Satan received permission from God to afflict Job and to strip him of all his property and riches. The Lord even allowed Satan to take Job's children, and eventually, his health. Surprisingly, it appears Job's suffering was God's idea. Notice in Chapter 1 that it was God who brought up Job's name in the conversation with Satan. God knew he could trust Job to bear up under the trials and even while suffering, to give a strong testimony. And indeed he did.

For thirty-five chapters, Job and his so-called friends debated God's role in Job's sufferings. Job protested that he didn't deserve all the loss and misery that had been inflicted on him by God, but he didn't rebel and curse God as his wife suggested. Job's friends, on the other hand, argued that God wouldn't have let all these bad things happen to him unless he deserved it. They insisted that Job had committed some pretty heinous sins for him to be punished so severely. Job didn't appreciate their accusations, and told them, *"Miserable comforters are you all. Will your long-winded speeches never end?" Job 16:2 (KJV)*

Job's ultimate conclusion after much agonizing over his fate, was to say pretty much what Habbakuk said, only in different words. *"Though he slay me, yet will I trust him." Job 13:15(KJV).* Job's testimony has glorified God down through the ages and ministered to us in the present age. Job's enduring faith was a defeat for Satan and a resounding victory for the kingdom of God. But, it took extreme suffering on Job's part to bring it to pass.

We wouldn't presume to compare ourselves with Job. Our family hasn't been through the tribulation fires to the extent Job was. However, the theme of Job's book and the lessons learned apply to our situation, and more broadly, to the suffering of all God's people. Job's losses led him to cry out to God all the more. There was no doubt in his mind God was there and he was controlling what was happening in Job's life. He just didn't understand why it had to be done that way and why it had to hurt so badly.

As a result of seeing how God used Job to further his kingdom work, we were greatly encouraged. Just as Satan had to get permission from God to afflict Job, we knew he also had to get permission from God before he could afflict and test us. Perhaps God would also use our suffering to glorify himself and further his kingdom's work. If these losses were all part of God's plan, then it would be worth all of the pain and suffering. Therefore, following Job's example, we too will trust God to the end, no matter what happens.

God spoke to Don through Job's cries for help as well as through his testimony of faith. We can see from Job's experience that it's all right to tell God how we feel, even if we feel angry or betrayed. He understands and can accept that and minister healing to us in the process. Even so, we must be careful not to accuse God of acting deceitfully or in bad faith for that would be to accuse him of sin. Unfortunately, Job crossed that line and had to be admonished by God. Even so, Job's questioning and God's responses demonstrated to us that it is okay to ask the hard questions. In the introduction to the book of Job in The Message Bible, Peterson has these words: "Every time we let Job give voice to our own questions, our suffering gains in dignity and we are brought a step closer to the threshold of the voice and mystery of God."

What are some of those questions? Well, why do sickness and afflictions have to come? Why do our loved ones have to die? Why do innocent children have seizures and why do they catch meningitis? And why do they die? Doesn't God care? Is he really in control? Does he intentionally cause these things to happen? Is the Evil One able to penetrate God's defenses and afflict God's people as he pleases?

People have asked these questions down through the ages and God has allowed them to be recorded in his Word. The Psalms, as well as the book of Job, are replete with them. God is not afraid of these questions. Surely he expects them from us. The only problem is, they are the wrong questions!

As Job told his wife, *"You are talking like a foolish woman. Shall we accept good from God and not trouble?"* Job 2:10

These questions seem reasonable from the human point of view, believing as we do in a God of love and justice. The problem is, the human viewpoint is very limited and cannot comprehend nor appreciate the infinite. God sees things in an eternal context and he controls them to bring about the greatest good for now and for eternity. What may now seem very hard and heartless may be necessary for God to accomplish a greater eternal purpose. As radio preacher Woodrow Kroll says, "Instead of asking *why*, it is better to ask *what now?*"

Holy Spirit Comfort

In the book of John we have the parting words of Jesus as he shared with his disciples just before his arrest and crucifixion. The disciples were distressed when Jesus told them he would be leaving them for a while. But more than that, Jesus knew that when he was crucified and they witnessed his death on the cross, they would be distressed and overcome by grief as their world seemed to tumble in on them. Jesus spoke to them in his compassion, saying *"Let not your hearts be troubled. You believe in God, believe also in me." John 14:1.* Then he promised them, *"If you love me, obey me; and I will ask the Father and he will give you another Comforter, and he will never leave you. He is the Holy Spirit, the Spirit who leads into all truth." John 14:15-17 (The Living Bible)*

God has given all Christians the wonderful gift of his Holy Spirit, the Comforter. The Greek word that is translated Comforter is Paraclete, meaning one who comes alongside to take up our cause. He wraps us in his loving arms and holds us close to his heart as he ministers to us from his unlimited love. The ministry of the Holy Spirit is the single greatest resource we have as we work our way through the grief process. Praise God for the provision of the Holy Spirit, our Comforter. If you are feeling alone and dejected in your pain, stop right now and go to your knees. Ask the Holy Spirit to help you and to give you his comfort. Ask him to come into your life and fill you with his presence. Ask him to fill every fiber of your being with his love and comfort. He will hear your prayer and come in to you, and hold you close in his loving arms. He will never leave you nor forsake you.

If you are not currently a Christian, you too can receive the comfort of the Holy Spirit. It's just a matter of accepting and believing. You see, the Holy Spirit is simply the spirit of Christ who has been promised to all who accept Christ into their hearts. You can do that right now by simply praying to Jesus to come into your heart and forgive you of your sins. The Bible says that *"God so loved the world that he gave his only son (Jesus) that whoever believes in him would not perish but receive eternal life" John 3:16.* It's that simple.

Lifeworthy Saints

W e have established that first of all God loves us, he knows and feels our emotions, and he cares about what happens to us. He has provided his people, his Word and now he has provided the Comforter, his Holy Spirit to come into us and minister to our pain. Now let us look at the way he has created us to be able to cope with the storms of life, even though we must endure the pain of separation. He has done a wonderful job of creating us to be resilient in the face of loss. Don likes to call the way God made us "Lifeworthy". This term is a takeoff from his experience in the Navy where the nautical term, "Seaworthy" is used. A seaworthy ship is designed and built to survive the worst storms it is expected to see on the high seas. Those storms can be overwhelming, as Don experienced during his days in the Navy. But, the seaworthy ship fights her way through them and survives. God has designed and built us to survive the most difficult storms of life. We may take a beating, but ɘp fighting through the waves of grief that threaten to overwhelm us.

While our daughter Rachel was fighting for her life in the intensive care ward after contracting meningitis, we met a remarkable person in the hospital waiting room. Ellen was a young mother, probably in her early thirties, with five small children. Her husband was in a coma as a result of an automobile racing accident and he was not expected to live. Ellen was an attractive and articulate woman, amazing in many ways. As we waited the long night out together in the hospital, the lives of our loved ones hung in the balance. We talked throughout the night, sharing our concerns and our anxieties. Ellen said something very profound that night. When we asked her what she would do if her husband died, she replied with confidence, "You know, the human spirit is very strong. The loss of a loved one can be devastating, but God has made us so we can handle it. We will survive, and we will be all right."

Ellen taught us an important lesson. She helped us realize God created us to be remarkably resilient beings. God has indeed made us lifeworthy to cope with and endure whatever life brings our way. Ellen was sure people could survive and recover from almost anything, given time and faith in God. Even though the death of a child or a spouse seems to us to be more than we can bear, we can survive. And not just survive, but recover fully! We will heal and we will be able to enjoy life again. God has made it possible through his mercy and grace.

Death and dying truly are integral parts of our lives. God created us to live and function in a world where people die. Some of those people are going to be ones we love. He has equipped us to be able to cope with the death of loved ones, and to go on living. In our minds we can imagine nothing worse than a loved one dying, and perhaps there is nothing more sorrowful. When it happens, however, we survive. With God's help we cope. We go on living and we recover. We may not feel we want to at times, but we do what we have to do.

A trauma to the soul is not much different from a physical trauma such as a disease or a broken bone. The body is equipped with an autoimmune system that causes the body to heal itself. Bones heal just as cuts and bruises do. It just takes time and care. It's the same with the human psyche. The pain of grief is severe and God knows that, but the pain is also transient. The wounded soul heals with time if we will let it. God brings healing in time, and strength and comfort in the meantime. We will find happiness, joy and meaning again in our lives.

We don't know how Ellen came to have so much wisdom for such a young lady. We have always suspected she was an angel in disguise, sent to minister to us. While we were talking to Ellen, her husband's doctor came into the waiting room and announced to her that her husband had just expired. We wept with her and then she gathered her things and walked out of our lives as abruptly as she entered. While we never saw her again, we did keep track of her for a few years through mutual friends we learned of during our vigils. We learned that her strength and faith did indeed see her through that crisis. Her life stabilized again and a few years later she remarried. Her five children had a father again. She was right. We mortal human beings, created in the image of God, can with faith and determination recover from almost anything.

Without a relationship with God, however, recovery must be much more difficult. Unfortunately, even some Christians do not find the peace God has provided in their time of sorrow. Even though the Holy Spirit is there to provide strength, courage, comfort and even a deep well-spring of joy that seems completely out of place, they do not allow him to work in their lives. They seem to prefer to suffer, although that is not God's plan for us. We are not left alone to cope with this most deep and profound emotion. How we pity those who must undergo this process without God in their lives, and without close family and friends to support them.

Expressing Our Grief

Now let's look at some things we can do to help ourselves as we navigate these painful waters. We all feel tremendous emotions in the time of grief and it is important to express these emotions in order to find release and healing. We need to cry. As we mentioned earlier, the Bible even records Jesus being moved by grief. It says in the book of John, *"When Jesus saw her weeping, and the Jews who had come along with her also weeping, he was deeply moved in spirit...and Jesus wept. John 11:33*

Don't worry about looking weak to others. They don't want you to hold in your grief for their benefit, or for the benefit of your vanity. You can always ask to be alone for a while if necessary, where you can cry out to God for his help, and let it all out. You will need to cry a lot in the early days and perhaps even weeks. The venting of our emotions is essential. It is actually harmful to try to hold your emotions in, for whatever reason. Repressed grief finds its way out eventually, and it can be manifested in unpleasant ways.

Even though we tried to deal with our grief outwardly and apparently did some things right, there was still some repressed emotion. You know how we are. We feel we have to be a rock for the family and demonstrate our strength to others around us. We did some of that, I'm sure, although we cried together many times. But for a long time afterward, months and maybe even a year or two later, we would both find ourselves feeling uneasy without any apparent reason. Don would tense up and maybe even feel angry and lash out at our girls, which was very unusual for him. He's always been an easy-going guy and felt blessed that he didn't get upset as easily as other men we know. Each time we prayed about this problem, we got subtle reminders that what we had been through with the children wasn't going to go away immediately. We needed to keep talking it out with each other and the girls, and even close friends we could confide in. Apparently it was an indication that our psyches were not completely healed yet.

Another way we can express our grief is through writing a journal. There is something therapeutic about writing down your thoughts. Don began writing a couple of weeks after Beth died, remembering all the things about Beth that we loved and didn't want to forget. He wrote about how he was feeling physically and emotionally. He wrote whatever came into his mind and it helped both of us to heal as we read through what had been written and talked about it. Much of what he wrote in his journal eventually found its way into our companion book, "Grace Enough for Three".

Whether you write or not, it is good for tears to flow freely as broken hearts express their agony in the language of sorrow and grief. The more we cry in the early day, the sooner the grief will subside. Besides crying, that may mean talking to people about what has happened and what we are feeling. That is the necessary process that leads to healing and recovery. Everyone needs to find that expression. The first loss we experienced with Mike left us dismayed and confused. We needed to talk about it with someone and try to find some meaning in it all. However, most of our friends and family members tried to get our minds off of our grief by talking to us about other things. But what we really needed to do was talk about what we were feeling. They would be talking on about something or the other and our minds would be miles away, thinking about Mike. In our subsequent losses we learned to tell people straight out that we wanted to talk about what was going on in our souls, and usually our friends and family were happy to go there with us.

Now I want to issue a warning at this point. While crying is good in the early days, continuous crying for weeks and months after your loss can be unhealthy and a sign that you are not healing properly. I know people who still cry at the drop of a hat years after their loss, indicating something has gone awry in the healing process. That leads us to the next subject, which is the need for self control and mental discipline as time goes on.

Mental Discipline

While we don't need to be worrying about ministering to other people in our early grief, we do have a responsibility to ourselves. It's hard, but even in our pain we need to exercise some mental discipline. One of the greatest battles in the grief process is enduring the pain of the realization that we have also lost our plans for the future, as well as our loved one. A lot of the distress of grief is the pain caused by thinking and fretting about the future. "What about all the many things we had planned to do together? It will be so hard to live without him or her; I don't think I can do it." You may think you can't live without him or her and you dread the prospect of not having that loved one around. But you really need to tell yourself, "I'm not going to worry about tomorrow or the next day. I won't let myself think about all of the plans we had made and all we were looking forward to together." Remember your loved one is in a much better place, in perfect health and enjoying the presence of God. As

Jesus was preparing to leave his disciples, he told them *"If you loved me, you would be glad I am going to the Father."* John 14:28

Our loved one is fine and enjoying Heaven, but we must suffer the grief of being left behind. So, we tend to feel sorry for ourselves and worry about how hard it will be. You mustn't think and worry about how hard it will be in the future. We repeat, it is not healthy to worry and fret about the future. Exercise some discipline and don't let your mind go there. God gives us grace to endure what's going on in our lives right now. He doesn't give us grace for the future until the future gets here. So here's what you must do. Just love Jesus and trust him to take care of you moment by moment. That is the most important thing. It is the essential thing. God will allow us to heal before he asks more of us. Remember, Jesus said, *"Peace I leave with you. My peace I give you.... Do not let your hearts be troubled and do not be afraid"* John 14:27.

We learned this lesson with our brain-damaged daughter, Rachel. As she continued to grow physically, it was getting more difficult to carry her around, and to get her to church where the ladies were graciously willing to watch her in the nursery. We began to worry about what was going to happen when she got too big to carry around. We didn't know what we were going to have to do and that worried us. While Don was praying about the situation one day, he felt God saying to him, "Why are you worrying about the future? Am I not taking care of you now?" Don said, "Yes Lord, right now things are fine. But what about when she gets too big?" God asked him again, "Am I taking care of you right now?" Don said, "Yes, but...". God said again, "Am I taking care of you right now?" Finally Don began to get the message. He said, "Yes Lord, you are taking care of us right now in a wonderful way, and now I realize you will take care of us in the future, just as you are now."

We began to see that it was like the Hebrew children in the wilderness. God provided manna for them each day, but only enough for that day. If they tried to gather enough for the next day or two, it would spoil and be inedible. God gave them their daily bread and they had to trust him for the days ahead. Jesus taught us in the Lord's Prayer to ask for our daily bread, not for a week's supply. It's the same with our other needs. We need to trust God daily for his sufficient grace, not fretting about whether it will be there tomorrow. That's the mental discipline we're talking about.

In the fourth chapter of the book of Philippians, the Apostle Paul gives us some good advice about exercising mental discipline. His mind may have been on some other problems of wrong thinking, but his advice certainly is appropriate to our situation. He counseled the Philippians, *"Do not be anxious about anything, but in everything by prayer and petition, with thanksgiving, present your requests to God. And the peace of God, which transcends all understanding, will guard your hearts and your minds in Christ Jesus" Philippians 4:6-7.*

In other words, God's peace is supernatural because it's not part of our normal response to losing someone. We shouldn't be feeling peace in our hearts when we are torn up inside. But that peace is real and it is predicated on your prayers and petitions, not forgetting to express thanksgiving in the process. Yes, there is much to be thankful for, even when you are grieving. As the old hymn says, "Count your blessings". Then Paul said, *"Think about these things."* In other words, instead of letting your mind dwell on what might have been, or how hard it is going to be without him or her, think about these things: *"Whatever is true, whatever is noble, whatever is right, whatever is pure, whatever is lovely, whatever is admirable – think about such things."*

Paul says, when you find yourself beginning to feel sorry for yourself and your heart begins again to ache when you think of your (seemingly) empty future, exercise some mental discipline and think about something else. Think about something lovely or true or beautiful in your life. We might begin with positive thoughts about the blessings God has given us and build on them. Think about your family and friends who are still around you and thank God for them. Think about the love of God and his promises to keep us in his care. Tell him how you are feeling and ask for his help. Surely there are some people still in your life who you love and enjoy. Think about them. Think about those lovely grandchildren or some of the great memories from your past. Be in control of your mind. It may seem to have a will of its own, wanting to worry about the future, but you don't have to allow that to happen. It won't do a bit of good and may cause your grief to intensify when it should be getting better.

In our experience the process follows a general time line if we face our grief in a positive way with dependence on God. Remember the nautical comparison we discussed earlier when we coined the term lifeworthy? We can use that analogy again because we found that grief is like waves breaking on the beach. A big wave comes in and pulls you under and you think you are going to be washed out to sea. But then that wave recedes and you feel like you're getting yourself back together, when another wave comes rolling in and knocks you down. But you get up again and soon another wave of grief washes over you, but then it recedes too. The waves keep coming but they are getting smaller and less forceful. The tide seems to be going out. Finally, the waves don't knock you down any more, and you begin to think you are past the worst of it. But then, the tide comes in again and you have to fight again to keep your head above water as the waves wash over your soul. But this time the waves aren't quite as forceful and you get through them without losing your equilibrium. And so the process continues until the waves become more manageable. Finally they just flow by softly, but still noticeable. But you know, we're not sure those waves ever go away completely. It has been decades now since we lost Mike, but on occasion we still feel a wave washing across our feet, reminding us of what we've lost.

Now, putting the grief process into real life terms, we can describe it in this way. At first we are overcome with grief and can do nothing but cry and cling to anyone or anything for help. It's hard to carry on a conversation without our minds wandering to our loss and ignoring everything else. After the funeral we begin the long process of grieving and working though the issues surrounding the loss. We fight through the waves of grief, but then something is said, or something reminds us of our loved one, and we are overcome again. As those battles continue, that's when we must begin to exercise our mental discipline. If we do, then within a few weeks we find our emotions stabilizing and we are able to function in public. Then after a few months we will find ourselves laughing and having fun again, even though our hearts may still ache when the laughter is over. You may feel that you could never get over your loss completely; you don't want to forget him or her and you will fight to keep your focus on them. But you can't live in your grief. It will destroy you. You will certainly never forget them and never lose the love you have for them. If you allow yourself, you can reach a point where your life gradually becomes normal.

Now there is an issue of timing here. We don't want to repress our emotions but at the same time we don't want to egg them on. There is a tendency to do that. We will deal with that more in the next chapter. One expert on grief has suggested it takes seven years to completely get over the death of someone very close. We can confirm that assessment in our own lives. Don says that for several years after we lost Beth, he thought he would never be able to feel deep emotion again. Experiences which before had brought tears to his eyes, or excitement to his soul, were now bland and plain. But after a few more years he was surprised one day to find a lump in his throat and tears in his eyes during a beautiful worship service. Since that day, he has found himself returning more and more to a full emotional life. He was even surprised recently to find himself wiping away tears during a sappy love movie. Yes, joy does come in the morning. Life can be beautiful again.

The term "bittersweet" is often used to describe the feeling of grief. It was appropriate for us because the acute pain of grief was mixed with the loving memories of joy and happiness each of our children brought into our lives. We wanted to think about them constantly and remember the love and joy they brought into our lives. That is the sweet part and it's okay to spend time thinking about those memories. And yet every thought brought pain and heartache because they were lost to us and that's what made the experience bitter. But, the good thing is that the bitter part fades with time while the sweet part stays with us for life.

The Sin of Self Pity

The loss of a loved one is surely one of the most difficult things in life to endure. We know God provides the helps we have discussed already to minister to us in our grief. If we allow him to, the Lord will move us through the grief process in a reasonable length of time. Even so, it is never easy. It hurts. It hurts terribly. Grieving is hard work, and it is often messy. We may blubber all over ourselves and find it makes us say and do things that are inappropriate. But, as we stated earlier, the fact we allowed ourselves to love someone makes the task necessary. It is an arduous task but not an impossible one. We need to recognize and accept the fact it is going to be a difficult job. Then we need to face it like any hard job and tackle it head on. God has equipped us to handle the job and he will be there to help us through it. In 1 Corinthians 10:13, the apostle Paul writes, *"No trial has taken you except what is common to man. And God is faithful; he will not let you be tried beyond what you can*

bear. But when you are tried, he will also provide a way out so that you can stand up under it."

The word for trial is usually translated as temptation, but it can apply to both. The message is that God will not put more on a person than he can take, and (this is a very important *and*) he will provide all the necessary help to ensure you can make it through. This verse isn't just talking about resisting temptations to sin. It also applies to the trial of sorrow. God will not put more on you than you can endure.

There is a powerful temptation to sin associated with the grief situation. The temptation is to become immersed in our sorrow and never recover. We can easily begin feeling sorry for ourselves and let the devil gain the victory. Our judgment can become clouded and we can become irrational in our behavior. That in turn can transition into clinical depression, and depression can end up in thoughts of suicide. Maybe that is why God gave us this passage in Jeremiah. *"Rachel is weeping for her children and she cannot be comforted, for they are gone. But the Lord says; "Don't cry any longer, for I have heard your prayers and you will see them again." Jeremiah 31:15-16 (KJV)*

King David illustrated how this behavior can affect even the best of us. When his son Absalom was killed, he continued to mourn for him incessantly, crying *"O my son Absalom! My son, my son Absalom! If only I had died instead of you - O Absalom, my son, my son"* 2 Samuel 18:33.

Joab, the general of David's army, had to come to him and essentially slap him around in order to bring him to his senses. He needed to see his ceaseless mourning was communicating to his troops that they didn't matter. Only his evil son Absalom mattered to him. In time God may say to us, it is time to stop mourning, or rise above it, and get on with your life. There is more work for you to do. But, he never says that until he knows we are ready and the time is right. We may never feel the time is right if it were left up to us, but if we keep our eyes focused on the Lord, he will bring us out of overwhelming sorrow and set us on our feet again.

There is another interesting example from the Old Testament. The prophet Samuel was mourning for King Saul when God said to him *"How long will you mourn for Saul, since I have rejected him as king over Israel? Fill your horn with oil and be on your way..."* 1 Samuel 16:1. God has work for us to do and does not intend for us to spend the rest of our lives grieving. He will sustain us and give us new energy and enthusiasm for life as we trust him and look to him daily for strength and guidance.

Jesus himself identified self-pity as originating with Satan when he admonished Peter for tempting Him to put his own feelings above his mission. He said, *"Get behind me Satan. You are a stumbling block to me; you do not have in mind the things of God but the things of men" Matthew 16:23.*

We can get some insight into how God works to bring us out of our sorrow through a paraphrase of the 'Sufficient

Grace' passage in 2 Corinthians 12:7-10. Equating the pain of our loss to the pain Paul experienced with his 'thorn in the flesh', the Message Bible addresses our grief situation this way. *"Satan's angel did his best to get me down; what he in fact did was push me to my knees. No danger then of walking around high and mighty! At first I didn't think of it as a gift, and begged God to remove it. Three times I did that, and then he told me, My grace is enough; it's all you need. My strength comes into its own in your weakness. Once I heard that, I quit focusing on the hardship and began appreciating the gift. It was a case of Christ's strength moving in on my weakness. Now I take limitations in stride, and with good cheer, these limitations that cut me down to size …. I just let Christ take over! And so the weaker I get, the stronger I become."*

Grief As Spiritual Warfare

In Jesus' "High Priestly Prayer" in John 17, Jesus petitioned the Father to protect his followers from "the evil", or some translate it, from "the Evil One". Also, in the model prayer Jesus instructed us to pray *"deliver us from evil"*. How can we interpret the death of our loved ones in the light of this prayer of our Savior? If the Father ever heard and answered a prayer, it must have been this prayer of his church and his only Son. Does evil triumph when a loved one is taken from us suddenly? Did the Evil One have his way when Beth had her accident? Did God lose control?

Our answer is no! As God gave Satan permission to afflict Job, God allowed these things to happen to our children within his purpose and in his will. We can't answer the "why" questions, and even asking them is fruitless. Frequently there are feelings of guilt in the early stages of grief, but we can't heal properly if we keep worrying over what we could have done differently. We may keep asking ourselves, "What if we hadn't been where we were", or "what if I'd gotten my child to the hospital sooner", or a million other "what ifs? We must exercise that self discipline and keep those thoughts out of our consciousness and just rest assured that God is in control.

God's permissive will sometimes allows earthly life to end early in difficult ways. However, God is still triumphant. The child or the older Christian may join the Father in heaven a few years earlier than we expected, and for them that is wonderful. He eternally multiplies their joy with him. We who are left behind suffer the pain of the loss. But, as we have discussed before, God will use our suffering to personally strengthen us and to accomplish his will in his kingdom's work. We have the love and support of family and friends to help us through. We can come through this time of pain and grief with our faith intact and, as my family learned, even strengthened.

There is a strong parallel between resisting temptation to sin, and withstanding the trials and testing of grief and bereavement. In both cases, the Lord has provided the means for us to withstand the onslaughts. That doesn't mean he will automatically fight our battles for us. He expects us to be involved in fighting our own battles, using the training and equipment which he has provided for us. Yet, even so, he promised us *"Never will I leave you; never will I forsake you"* Hebrews *13:5.* He will see us through.

In Ephesians 3:16 Paul prays for us a very important prayer. *"That He may strengthen you with power through His*

Spirit in your inner being, so that Christ may dwell in your hearts through faith. And... that you, being rooted and established in love, may have power... to grasp how wide and long and high and deep is the love of Christ." Later in Ephesians, Paul explains to us the fact we are in spiritual warfare. *"For our struggle is not against flesh and blood, but against the rulers, against the authorities, against the powers of this dark world and against the spiritual forces of evil in the heavenly realms" Ephesians 6:12.* Then he lists some of the provisions God has made available to us to help us in that warfare. He says *"Therefore, put on the full armor of God, so that when the day of evil comes, you may be able to stand your ground" Ephesians 6:13.* Again, he says to be equipped *"so when the day of evil comes, you may be able to stand your ground".*

To some degree at least, these words are the answer to Jesus' high priestly prayer for the Father to *"protect them from the evil".* God provides us with protection by strengthening us in our inner person with his Spirit as we spend time with him in his Word, in prayer, and in service, building our "spiritual muscles". Then, he goes on to equip us for battle with the "Armor of God". Paul lists the pieces of God's armor. He describes the helmet of salvation, the breastplate of righteousness, the belt of truth, and the shoes of peace. In addition, he says, *"... take up the shield of faith with which you can extinguish all the flaming arrows of the evil one. Take... the sword of the Spirit, which is the Word of God, and pray in the Spirit on all occasions" Ephesians 6:16.*

We hope you can see how this teaching applies to the grief situation. Again, this passage is often applied in relation to fighting the desires of the flesh, and perhaps has never been thought of as applying to the grief problem. While the situations are quite different, there are also many similarities. The Evil One will attack us whenever and wherever he can find an opening. He has no mercy. The fact that we are hurting and devastated with grief doesn't deter him from the attack. He delights to kick us when we're down and vulnerable. We see that clearly in the case of Job. Actually, Satan probably feels he has a better chance for victory when we are down than at any other time. He always attacks the weakest area of our lives, the chink in our armor, at the most opportune time for him. That is logically the worst time for us.

It is true that tragic losses do indeed turn some people away from God and Satan wins that battle; but not necessarily the war. It seems that people either turn to God for strength and comfort, or else they blame him and become bitter and estranged from him. If the Evil One can't turn us against God, he may try another tack and try to steal our joy by leading us to wallow in self pity or guilt, delaying our recovery as long as possible. We can just see Satan sympathizing with a grieving Christian and saying "You poor thing, you must feel awful. Go ahead and feel sorry for yourself, you have every right too. God shouldn't have let this terrible thing happen to you."

Some people do give up and waste away in their sorrow until their own lives are gone. In those cases, the evil one again wins a victory. It isn't because God didn't answer Jesus' prayer for us, however. It's because people fail to avail themselves of the ample provisions the Father has made for us so *"when the day of evil"* comes, we will be ready.

It doesn't seem fair that a person who is crushed with grief should have to stand up and fight the evil one in his or her day of greatest need. In a sense they don't have to if they are properly prepared. Paul prayed for us to be strengthened in our inner person, and to put on the full armor of God, so that *when* the day of the evil comes, we will be able to withstand. So, if we are spiritually prepared, we will be able to stand when that day comes, even in our weakened condition.

The message here is not to wait until the day of testing and trial comes to begin preparing for it. We shouldn't wait until the house is on fire to begin reading the instructions for operating the fire extinguisher. Get ready now! Develop your spiritual muscles, and put on the whole armor of God now. Don't let the Evil One catch you unprepared. Unless you die first, you will eventually experience the loss of one of your closest loved ones. Will you be ready? Have you made preparation? Are you strengthened in your "inner man"? Are you equipped with the full armor of God?

We can defeat the enemy if we stay rooted in Christ. In the book of James it tells us if we resist the devil, he will flee from us. We say now, based on what we believe God showed us, if you resist Satan with the Word of God, he will crawl away from you, face down in the dirt.

So, our premise is, the devil can use the grief situation to attack God's children and try to turn us from our faith in God. On the night before his crucifixion, the Lord told Peter, *"Simon, Simon, Satan has asked permission to sift you like wheat, but I am praying for you that your faith will not fail" Luke 22.* Notice that Jesus didn't say he was praying for Peter to be spared the sifting. No, he said "I am praying for you that your faith will not fail." Jesus knew that Peter would be tested and that he would fail. But he didn't want Peter to give up and lose his faith so he prayed to the Father that Peter's faith would survive. As we know, it did, because Jesus later commissioned him to minister to the church and he did so in great power. God allowed our family to be sifted like wheat, but he never left us. We know in our hearts that Jesus was praying for us that our faith would not fail. And it hasn't. In fact, our faith is stronger now than it has ever been, and the trials we went through actually strengthened our faith. That's definitely God's grace at work.

Our advice here is that we should expect the attacks and be prepared to repel them. While we have said God expects us to fight our own battles with the provisions he has given us, we didn't say he would abandon us in our battles. No, he is there strengthening us and encouraging us. He will provide peace and understanding if we will let him. He knows we are hurting and not as able to fight as we normally are. He feels our pain and he understands. He will never leave us alone.

Some Practical Helps

In a practical sense we can help ourselves through the grief process by changing many of the habits we developed with the loved one who is gone. If we always went to certain places or did favorite things together, those places and things are always going to be painful in the future. We can work through those experiences in a brute force manner by continuing to do the same things and go the same places without the loved one. Eventually the painful association will fade. Alternatively, we can find new places to go and different things to do with other people. When our son Mike died, we relocated from California to Missouri and the dramatic changes along with the 'busyness' of the move helped us to move on much more quickly than if we had stayed in the same situation. Dramatic changes may not be possible for many people. That may be the more healthy approach, but it depends on your particular circumstances. You may not have the option if your circumstances are too restrictive.

Some of the most difficult times are the special days like Christmas and birthdays. Each special day without them will be very difficult the first time. For many years those special days will continue to be hard. To a degree, we simply have to "tough it out" and get through them. However, we can help ourselves by meeting each special day head on with a strategy. We tried to make plans that would surround us with friends and family, or would otherwise keep us too busy to dwell on the absence of our missing one. Since Rachel and Beth both died in the month of February, every year around that time we try to take a special vacation and get away from our normal routine. We indulge ourselves a little but we enjoy ourselves and keep our minds occupied with enjoyable activities. It really helps.

Once we have experienced each one of those special days in a different way without the missing one there, then the next time it will be a little easier. Even so, the special days and anniversaries will be somewhat difficult for several years. However, our loved ones would certainly prefer for us to observe those days with positive and constructive activities. They wouldn't want us to suffer unnecessarily by spending that day grieving and crying.

Clearly, one of the greatest difficulties in moving on is the emotional attachment to the loved one who is gone. When we find ourselves sinking in depression, that is the time to heed the Apostle's words and discipline our minds to think about other things. Remember we said we would think about things that are beautiful and healthy. But, even when we feel we are making progress in our grief, we may find ourselves not wanting to let go of their memory or anything that belonged to them. We feel we are being unfaithful to the one we have lost if we do anything to take our focus off their memory. That can be manifested by such things as refusing to clean out their closets and drawers or waiting indefinitely to change anything in their room. However, at some point, we have to let go of those things. It is extremely difficult to do it, but we must because those things constitute weights that hold us down and keep us from moving on to wholeness. If the task seems to daunting for you, it's all right to ask other family members to help you with it. The important thing is that it gets done.

We remember when we cleaned out Rachel's bureau drawers. We had waited a few weeks to do this heartbreaking task. Just seeing each of the little outfits she wore as we put her things away brought tears and aching hearts. But until we take those actions we can't move on with our lives. Those difficult and emotional tasks will always be haunting us and waiting for us until we get them done. Certainly, the one who is gone would not want us to waste our lives away by focusing constantly on their things, trying to hang on to what is gone. The good memories will still be there to be called up on occasions when it is appropriate. We have our favorite photographs of the children displayed in our home and a few favorite things the children made in a drawer somewhere.

We will never forget our children and the cherished memories of them if we live to be 100.

Of all the practical advice we can give regarding the grief process, the most important is to just lean on God and hold on. Spend time in God's Word, seeking out his many promises to us and taking strength from them. Again, we emphasize that God ministers to us through his Word. We spent hours and hours in the Bible after Beth's death, and God strengthened us and brought us comfort and understanding through that time with him. Call on the Holy Spirit as often as you need to. He'll always be there.

Don't be bashful about seeking out friends or family members to talk to or be with. If they don't come to you then you go to them. Most people want to help but many times they don't know how. If you just get in touch with them to talk, you may find you decide to do something together. Maybe you could go out to dinner or a show. You need to get out and attend social functions at church or other social circles where you are comfortable. That may be hard for you to do if you always did those things together before. But, you really need to get out in some way and not sit at home moping.

It is good to have friends and family who look after you and spend time with you. But, there are also times when you need to be alone. In Martha Whitmore Hickman's book, "I Will Not Leave You Desolate"[2] she writes "We should find some balance between solitude and socializing, both of which we need. People will urge socializing upon us. 'You need to get out,' they will say. We do need to get out in order to re-establish ourselves as persons who belong to life and to current relationships. But we also need time alone, to face our demons, to put down our plumb line and to take our soundings. We will probably cry and feel sad. We will also feel alive and enriched and less tense because we have looked our grief in the face, allowed our feelings to speak their authentic word. And when we move out again into the social world, it may be with a sense of having laid some burden down."

We mentioned earlier the benefits of writing down your thoughts. That may not work for everyone, but if you can do it, we're sure you will benefit from it. It is nature's way of helping to wipe away the sorrow from our mind, and transferring it to paper. But, no matter how resolved you are to make it through this personal loss, to some degree you are going to have to "tough it out" and do the work of grief. We can't escape the pain but it will get better in time. Our knowledge of God's sufficient grace gives us assurance throughout the ordeal that we will survive and there will be better days ahead. Not just by the intellectual knowledge that his grace is sufficient, but by the actual experiencing of that grace.

Each person in our family could feel the assurance and support of our heavenly Father as he carried us through those dark valleys. That grace continues to this day because his faithfulness to his children is eternal. Although we could not understand why we had to lose three children, we knew God was and is in control. We also know his will can never lead us where his grace will not keep us. That motto hangs on the wall in our home. We know it and believe it in our hearts and in our experience.

"The will of God will never lead you where the grace of God cannot keep you"

The ways of God are not easy for us to comprehend, but one thing we are sure of. No matter what pain we may undergo, the comforting words of Jesus are always there. He said *"Come unto me, all ye that labor and are heavy laden, and I will give you rest. Take my yoke upon you and learn from me, for I am gentle and humble in heart, and you will find rest for your souls. For my yoke is easy and my burden is light" Matthew 11:28-30.* One might question whether the burden is easy and light when we are suffering loss, but that's where his miraculous grace manifests itself.

Grief Lessons Learned

God taught our family many lessons through our children's sicknesses and deaths that we would never have learned otherwise. Many of them may seem self-evident but we think some of them may not be obvious until you think about them. Most of them are discussed in other sections of the book, or are treated in the companion book "Grace Enough for Three". However, we would like to summarize many of them here by way of recap and reminder. We've structured them sort of like the wisdom sayings in the book of Proverbs. These are the things we have learned and believe with all our hearts are true. We hope as you examine them you see some truth in them for yourself. We've tried to combine them into categories to help you deal with them. Here they are.

Category No. 1 - Reality – These lessons are just facts of life. Understanding them will help us to accept them as part of God's plan for all of us.

a. Living with death is a part of life. God has created and made us lifeworthy to cope with the death of ones close to us.

b. Death is a form of healing. We are all perfect in heaven.

c. Grieving is hard work. It is a difficult job but we can do it.

d. People deal with grief differently. People have to cope with grief in their own way.

e. Grief is most tolerable when we trust God completely and allow his goodness to comfort and guide us. He is the Great Comforter.

f. God rewards faithfulness. He will restore completely if we trust him completely.

g. We will see our loved ones again in Heaven. Years are but a blink of the eye in God's time.

h. Our young children who die are safe with God in heaven. They are dear to his heart.

Category No. 2 - God's Comfort - These lessons should help us to seek out and accept the comforts God provides for us.

a. Faith in God provides the power to go on through all trials, no matter how difficult. *"I can do everything through him who gives me strength" Philippians 4:13.*

b. One of the principal titles for the Holy Spirit is the Comforter. Call on Him often to come into your life and give you the comfort you need.

c. The Word of God is a great comfort as well as our rudder, pointing the way for us through life's trials. *"Your word is a lamp to my feet and a light for my path" Psalms 119:105.*

d. Comfort is ministered best through close personal relationships. Join a small group of some kind if you haven't already.

e. God is too good to be unkind. His compassion for us knows no bounds and he is in control.

f. God does not leave us alone to cope with this most deep and profound emotion in our own strength. He will never leave us nor forsake us.

Category No. 3 - Spiritual Warfare – These difficult lessons are also in the realm of reality but may be hidden from us.

a. The devil always attacks us at our weakest point. He has night-vision goggles to spot the chink in our armor.

b. The devil will take advantage of our emotional exhaustion to attack us. He has no mercy.

c. Don't let the evil one catch you unprepared. Begin now to prepare for your own experience with grief.

Develop your spiritual muscles and put on the whole armor of God.

d. Do not to give place to the devil by allowing habitual sin in your life. We give the devil a foothold in our lives when we sin willingly.

Category No. 4 - Practical Suggestions – Again, many of these concepts are commonly known but it helps to be reminded sometimes.

a. Writing down your thoughts during a time of sorrow is therapeutic. Start a Journal and write down the things about your loved one you do not want to forget.

b. Although we may feel we are being unfaithful to the one we have lost, at some point we have to let go of them (and their things) and get on with our lives. They would want us to.

c. A dramatic change of routine is very helpful in accelerating the healing process. Filling the mind with new and different experiences helps displace the recent memories of the loss.

d. When in sorrow, we must live in the present moment. We must not let ourselves dwell on what might have been…or what it will be like without our loved one. God is always taking care of us right now. He gives us grace for the present moment.

e. We can help ourselves get through holidays and other special days by meeting each special day head on with a strategy. Plan ahead.

Category No. 5 - Going Deeper With God. He doesn't just get us through our ordeals, he wants us to learn from them and go further in our love and devotion to him.

   a. Our grief can be used by God to strengthen us and prepare us for future service which will be profitable not only to us, but also to God's Kingdom and Glory.

   b. The way we handle our grief can be a strong testimony for God. People are watching.

   c. Total and complete surrender of our wills and our lives to God makes us usable to him. What can he do with our obedience?

   d. Feelings of love, peace and joy are what bring quality to life, and those things depend only on our fellowship with God.

   e. God may intentionally bring difficult and painful situations into our lives for his own purposes. We need to be able to accept that fact gracefully. His grace is sufficient.

   f. How we respond to the situations is what concerns our Lord. Jesus prayed that Peter's faith would not fail, not that he would be spared from Satan's sifting.

g. We may be called to suffer as Christians for the purpose of leading others to a saving knowledge of Jesus Christ.

h. God wants us to support his other children who are in grief. It is his intent that we be there, sharing our love and concern. We are his representatives.

i. The long-term need comes after the funeral when the crowd disappears. That is the loneliest time of the entire experience.

j. Don't tell God how to solve your problem (or anyone else's). Just share your concern with him and let him fix the problem his way.

k. Never pray for a specific course of action unless you are sure God is leading you.

l. God is too wise to be mistaken. His plan for us is good and the best thing for us.

m. We can be the happiest in the worst of circumstances when we let God have complete control. God can actually bring joy in the midst of great suffering.

n. More faith is required to trust God through difficulties than to pray for their removal. It's easy to pray for health, peace and prosperity.

o. God is looking for people who are willing to surrender everything to him, trusting him to use their obedience both for his kingdom and for them.

p. When we know God is in control, then regardless of the circumstances, "It is well".

Heaven

Perhaps the greatest comfort of all comes from the assurance that we will see our loved one(s) again in heaven. Our ideas of heaven are sometimes vague and misguided, but a recent book by Randy Alcorn has clarified and corrected many of those misconceptions. In his book entitled simply "Heaven" [3], Randy has devised a systematic treatment of the issues and parameters of heaven taken from many years spent in studying the Biblical teachings on heaven. Many of the best known and well educated theologians of our time have endorsed Alcorn's book as the best book ever written on the subject of heaven.

One of the most comforting teachings confirmed by Alcorn's book is that Christians will indeed be reunited with our loved ones who have gone on before us to heaven. Various opinions have been expressed that our entire being in heaven will be so immersed in worshipping God that we will not even be aware of other people. One recent widow reportedly said "If I can't be with my husband in heaven, I'm not sure I want to be there." The Bible, however, assures us that we will indeed be reunited with our loved ones and that we will be closer together than ever. Let me just quote a few passages from Alcorn's wonderful book.

"Paul tells the Thessalonians that we'll be reunited with believing family and friends in Heaven: *'Brothers, we do not want to you to be ignorant about those who fall asleep, or to grieve like the rest of men, who have no hope...God will bring with Jesus those who have fallen asleep in him...We who are still alive and are left will be caught up together with them...And so we will be with the Lord forever. Therefore encourage each other with these words'* (1 Thessalonians 4:13-14, 17-18). Our source of comfort isn't only that we'll be with the Lord in Heaven but also that we'll be with each other."(*p.342*)

Some argue that we will not remember or recognize each other in heaven. Alcorn writes, "What lies behind this question is the false assumption that in Heaven... we'll be disembodied spirits who lose our identities and memories. How does someone recognize a spirit?" Then he quotes J.C. Ryle who writes "The hope with which he (Paul) cheers wearied Christians is the hope of meeting their beloved friends again...But in the moment that we who are saved shall meet our several friends in heaven, we shall at once know them, and they will at once know us." Alcorn says "in fact, we'll have much less trouble. In Heaven we probably won't fail to recognize an acquaintance in a crowd, or forget people's names." (because our senses and memories will be enhanced). Alcorn then quotes missionary Amy Carmichael who had strong convictions on this point. "Shall we know one another in Heaven? Shall we love and remember? (*pp346-347*). I do not think anyone need wonder about this or doubt for a single moment. Would you be yourself if you did not love and remember?"

Alcorn uses his own family to illustrate the point. "Nothing will take away from the fact that Nanci and I are marriage partners here and that we invest so much of our lives in each other, serving Christ together. I fully expect no one besides God will understand me better (in Heaven), and there's nobody whose company I'll seek and enjoy more than Nanci's. The joys of marriage will be far greater because of the character and love of our bridegroom. I rejoice for Nanci and for me that we'll both be married to the most wonderful person in the universe. He's already the one we love most— there is no competition. On Earth, the closer we draw to him, the closer we draw to each other. Surely the same will be true in Heaven. People with good marriages are each other's best friends. There's no reason to believe they won't still be best friends in Heaven."(*p351*)

Then for people like Karen and Don, Alcorn has this to say. "What about our children? What about my relationship to my daughters and sons-in-law and closest friends? There's every reason to believe we'll pick right up in Heaven with relationships from Earth. We'll gain many new ones but will continue to deepen the old ones. The notion that relationships with family and friends will be lost in Heaven, though common, is unbiblical. It completely contradicts Paul's intense anticipation of being with the Thessalonians and his encouraging them to look forward to rejoining their loved ones in Heaven."*(p351)*

This is just a brief summary of some of the high points of the book "Heaven" that deal with the comfort of seeing and knowing our loved ones in heaven. The entire book would be great reading and encouragement for someone who is grieving a close loved one who has just made that journey to be with the Lord.

Conclusion

We hope this little book has given you some comfort, but more importantly we hope it has given you encouragement and some ideas of how you can approach the grief process more productively. For the reader who isn't sure that his or her position is secure with the Lord, you have hope also. You can know for certain by simply having a discussion with God right now, and telling him you want to be in relationship with him. He wants to accept you in his arms, especially if you are grieving and needing him in a special way. To enter into that relationship with him, it is only necessary that you ask him to come into your heart (which means your mind and your soul) accepting the sacrifice he made for you in the death and resurrection of Jesus Christ. God loved you so much that he sent his son Jesus to Earth as Immanuel, that is God With Us. The Bible says that if we confess with our mouths, and believe in our hearts that Jesus died for us, was resurrected on the third day, and ascended into Heaven, we will be saved. If you just tell him that you want to do that, you will be saved and become a born again child of God. As you come to God, you will see yourself as sinful and unclean, but that is part of the salvation process. Jesus died to take away your failings and mistakes. You only need to give him your heart and turn away from sin in your life. We pray you will take that step now and become a member of the family and find there the blessed comfort, love and acceptance you have been craving.

If you have found help in this little book, please let us know about it. Our e-mail address is <u>d.clifford@sbcglobal.</u><u>net</u>. We would love to hear from you. May God bless you richly. Amen

References

1. *C.S. Lewis Through the Shadowlands*, by Brian Sibley, Revell Publishers, 1994
2. *I Will Not Leave You Desolate*" by Martha Whitmore Hickman, Abingdon Press, 1994
3. *Heaven* by Randy Alcorn, Tyndale House Publishers, Carol Stream, Illinois, 2004

Printed in the United States
133803LV00001B/96/P